Rummle Them Up!
The Border Rugby Story

WALTER THOMSON
'Fly Half' of The Sunday Post

Foreword
BILL McLAREN

SPORTSPRINT PUBLISHING
EDINBURGH

To my favourite 'Rugby widow' and wife
GERDA

Text © Walter Thomson 1989

For assistance in the provision of illustrations
for this book, grateful thanks to:
Gordon Lockie and the *Southern Reporter*;
Bill McLaren; and Jim Telford.
And further thanks to Gordon Lockie
for the cover illustration.

ISBN 0 85976 287 4

Phototypeset by Beecee Typesetting Services
Printed in Great Britain by Bell & Bain Ltd., Glasgow

Foreword

IT seems in every sense appropriate that the significant stages in the progress of the Border Rugby game, its character and its personalities, should be thus recorded by Walter Thomson of Selkirk who first covered the Rugby scene as a reporter over 50 years ago and whose distinctive match reports, under the pseudonym 'Fly Half' in the *Sunday Post*, have been compulsive reading for generations of Borderers. Always fair, knowledgeable and objective in his assessments, he brings just those qualities to this fascinating series of recollections to provide another valuable addition to Rugby Union literature.

Borderers, and those furth of the district, will find much to stir the memory. Younger readers, too, will be encouraged towards a sense of pride in the achievements of their predecessors. The Border game, after all, blazed more than one trail. Every aspect has been covered from the earliest days to the creation of National Leagues, the tour games, the great players, the rivalries, the sevens and the lure of Rugby League. It is a story well worth the telling and Walter Thomson merits lasting appreciation for thus providing, with a light and humorous touch, such a riveting record of the Border Rugby game.

Bill McLaren

Contents

CHAPTER ONE

Why the Borders? How It Began

The mist of memory broods and floats
The Border waters flow,
The air is full of ballad notes
Borne out of long ago.

WILL Ogilvie was not thinking of Rugby when he wrote these lines. If he had, his finely tuned ear would have caught, amid the ballad cadences, the clash and clangour of byegone battles and the imploring call to 'Rummle them up', that Border version of the national invocation 'Feet, Scotland, Feet!'

I hope to rummle up a few memories as I sift through random recollections of more than half-a-century of observing the Rugby scene from the sanctuary of the press-box. I have lost count of the number of Border games I have covered in addition to around a couple of hundred internationals and many major representative games, the ubiquitous 'sevens' and — whisper it — even a women's Rugby League match played within the hallowed confines of the Borders.

But why the Borders anyway? What is so special about this lovely but thinly populated corner of the country that it should so resolutely reject the likes of its 'fitba' daft' neighbours and choose to play with an oval ball and to a code, let's not deny it, that originated on the playing field of an English public school? For a district which determinedly guards its marches and commons and defies the invader from across the Border, that seems a contra-diction in attitude and it is worth enquiring why.

1

Some writers have tried to rationalise what on the face of things must have been an unlikely preference. It was a fateful choice too because over the decades this small enclave of Scotland has regularly claimed around half of the places in the national XV, and sometimes a bigger chunk than that. When the Scottish Rugby Union centenary was celebrated with an international seven-a-side tournament at Murrayfield in 1973, to whom did the selectors turn? Not to a representative spread from the original or oldest clubs in membership but to the Borders for the entire seven, and calling on only two clubs, Hawick and Gala, to provide the men. Not bad coming from a population of 100,000, a tiny minority of whom still, perversely, choose to kick a spherical ball around.

The Borders have been likened to South Wales as a bastion of Rugby, but in Wales numbers are concentrated in the valleys and steel towns and cities. In Scotland it is the other way round. The Rugby backbone reaches through the rural areas. There is a whiskered jest about a game on a Border ground which had gone disastrously contrary to at least one spectator's expectations. 'Cheer up,' said his neighbour, 'It's hardly a matter o' life and death.' 'No,' came the dejected rejoinder, 'it's mair serious than that.'

Some historians have sought to establish an affinity between present-day Rugby and the games which were played in the Borders in mediaeval times and even by the Roman centurions camped within kicking distance of the Greenyards at Trimontium. I don't believe a word of it. The most enduring of bloodthirsty theories is that Rugby is some sort of cleaned up version of an activity once popular in the wake of a cross-border sortie in Jedforest. They applied their own form of 'Jethart Justice'. It was a case of 'off with their heads and we'll try them later'.

These severed heads, so the legend goes, were adopted by the local callants for a passing, kicking game between such ancient adversaries as the Uppies and the Doonies. It is still played in the barricaded streets of Jedburgh at Candlemas and Fasterne'en and it lingers on in the odd Border village. Melrose kept up the custom with a 'marriage ba'' where the bride kicked off in the Market Square and traffic ground to a halt. I remember a worthy minister, the late Rev. Harry Dodd, top hat and all, joining exuberantly in the game. But then he was a Jethart man and old habits die hard, even at a wedding reception.

The most impressive recent enactment of a Border ba' took place at Bowhill, the ancestral home of the Dukes of Buccleuch. It was intended to show how the game was played in 1815, well before a certain English public schoolboy picked up the ball and ran with it at Rugby. The original pitch at Carterhaugh was brought back into use. Two Dukes encircled the arena, ducal pennons fluttering, just as when Sir Walter Scott presided over the 1815 game. The Border clubs of today provided the players and I am bound to say that some of them enjoyed themselves as never before. There was no referee and rules seemed to be invented as play went along.

In one respect the 1815 match was not followed up because, one greatly regrets to place on record, this Border ba' of nearly two centuries ago produced one of the first recorded cases of football hooliganism. Well, perhaps that is too strong a word. At one point in the afternoon some players changed sides and the result was hotly disputed. Sir Walter Scott's carriage was stopped by an angry mob in Selkirk's Market Place as the great man made his way home to Abbotsford. Showing more perspicacity than some modern referees might have displayed in the circumstances, he disarmed the rioters by tossing them a few guineas at which they promptly disappeared into the nearest alehouse, no doubt to sing the early nineteenth-century equivalent of Rugby songs.

Having seen this Carterhaugh re-enactment and watched the odd heaving scuffle in the streets of Jedburgh, I feel bound to say that I am not convinced that there is a link between the two games. Much more likely that Rugby was brought to the Borders by the early entrepreneurs of the tweed and hosiery industries who had played a bit in England before expanding textiles in the district. It was only after they came that you could tell you were in the Borders by the tall mills, and the H-shaped goalposts.

Probably the first town to experience this industrial and sporting awakening was Langholm. As early as 1871 they were playing regular fixtures. Two years later they inaugurated what they claim as the first club 'international', playing Carlisle on the

Castleholm. One would like to record a milestone victory for one country or the other but this would be dubious. At that time Rugby had not yet been trimmed to fifteen-a-side. Langholm were fielding 20 players but Carlisle arrived with 25 and argument flew thick and fast before the game even kicked off. Langholm finally established the point that as they owned the ball they had the right to make the rules. Very late, play began. As darkness closed in the ball was lost. A draw claimed Carlisle, a win claimed Langholm — because they were leading. Now we shall never know.

CHAPTER TWO

Early Days: Some Surprising Firsts

RUGBY plainly filled a sizeable gap in the Border way of life from the 1870s onwards. The old unruly handba' jousts were shedding their appeal. Early sporting fixtures such as archery contests for assorted antique silver arrows were withering. There was cricket, it was true, transplanted to the Borders with considerable success from the 1830s and capable at one time of challenging Rugby for crowd appeal and Scottish caps. Not even musclebound Borderers, however, could be persuaded to settle little local difficulties over a cricket pitch in midwinter. No, it had to be Rugby, sleeves rolled up, shorts warming the knees and fiercely partisan spectators rallying behind the combatants.

Argument was fuelled as much by confusion over the laws of the game as by anything that happened on the pitch. Borderers always did enjoy passionate debate, whether on politics or the true worth of penalty goals. Rugby provided the perfect platform.

The clubs began in much the same way, though with the inevitable local variations. In Hawick, for instance, two clubs flourished side by side, providing the kind of domestic rivalry of the old-style Uppies and Doonies, or East and West-enders. These two were Hawick and St Cuthbert's, akin to Hawick and Wilton on the cricket field, and amicable marriage was ultimately consummated. It does not seem to have been quite such a platonic affair at Gala where an informal liaison with Melrose was rudely interrupted by a takeover bid which proceeded under cover of darkness and saw goalposts and club colours removed to the Greenyards overnight — a *fait accompli* worthy of your modern City mogul. Gala quickly discovered that a state of single bliss was not without its advantages and they soon built up a new club on the windy heights of Mossilee, losing nothing by the deal, apparently, except jerseys and goalposts. Melrose, to be fair, reimbursed Gala with a new set of posts, but they took an unconscionable time to do it, a hundred years in fact, the gesture being made when the two committees got together over a friendly pint to recall their joint beginnings. Gala thrived on their own. They rivalled Hawick as the main town in the Borders and they were soon recognised as the 'Big Two'.

One of the things which never fails to astonish me is the enterprise and ingenuity which was shown by these pioneers of the Border clubs. They were far ahead of their time. Just think of the gamble which Hawick took in 1879 when they organised the 'Electric Light Match', the first floodlit fixture in Scotland. They had no money in the bank and floated a limited liability company to finance this single game, having no wish thus early to bankrupt the emerging Greens. Electric light was a great novelty. Many paid their way in to see this latest wonder of science as much as to watch a full-blooded match between Melrose and Hawick.

Hawick picked up the idea from a moderately successful experiment in Sheffield — the old Yorkshire connection — a few weeks earlier. The date was set for a wintry night in February. Special trains brought spectators from all over the district. It was estimated that there was a crowd of over 5,000. As to that, no one could be sure. The generators were not due to start up until play began, so followers stumbled through the night to find the trestle table, equipped with oil-lamp, where the gatekeeper presided. In the crush he and his earthenware bowl were overturned. One would not like to whisper it within earshot of Whitehall that this could have been another first in sporting hooliganism! Over-exuberance, surely, but no more!

It must have been a weird sight which rewarded those who had paid — or scrambled — their way in. Generators were set up at either end of the pitch, producing an effect like the confetti of hand-cranked home movies. Curious spectators kept getting in

How Border Rugby looked in the old days, with shorts down to the knees succeeding longs which lapped over the ankles. This was taken at a Melrose-Hawick game when spacing at the line-out was evidently not of crucial importance.

the way of the beam, eager to see where this miraculous light was coming from, and throwing bizarre shadows against the snow. Perhaps this was when shadow tackling began. To put the peter on a hilarious night the economical operators shut down their generators the moment the referee blew no-side, which left bleary-eyed players and spectators to stumble their way to baths or the nearest bar as best they could.

The original 'Electric Light Match' can hardly have been written off as a total disaster because Kelso employed the same generators a few weeks later to shed light on a match at Springwood. After that a blackout descends on the Border Rugby scene until Kelso, imaginatively, brought back floodlighting to the district with a system, since much improved, which was installed at Poynder Park in the 1960s. This has been a boon to the district, enabling representative matches at all levels to be played off when dates would otherwise have been difficult to find.

If electric light was one stunning piece of Border Rugby innovation in the formative years, what of their invitation to the first overseas team to reach the U.K.? This was the original Maoris of 1888-89, forerunners of the mighty All Blacks, and a remarkable venture by any yardstick, not least the nine months the players were away from home. Their single appearance in Scotland was made at the invitation of the Hawick club. These strange dark-skinned Rugby players from afar made a huge impression and spectators flocked to Mansfield from all over the area — dare one say, as much to see Maoris as to watch Rugby?

It must have been quite a match. I would love to have covered it. The Maoris won by a goal to a try but only after some mesmeric passages of play by the tourists and some stonewall tackling by Hawick. Even if it was a little before my time I have had the good fortune to interview someone who played in it and who retained the souvenirs to prove it. Tom Riddle, Hawick's full back in the match, was among the guests half a century later when New Zealand met the South. He told me about an incident which passed into folklore.

The Maoris, athletic, inventive, as now, had one star, a wing who was so fast and so elusive that no one, it was said, in the earlier games in England and Wales had been able to lay a finger on him. Tom did. Not only that, but when despatched clean away from deep in his own half this twinkling little fellow even had the cheek to blow a kiss to the opposing full back who was just over the horizon. That triggered a tackle which reverberated round the Borders for many a day, right up, I should say, till another Hawick full back felled a Springbok wing of the 1930s. Riddle got the Maori in his sights as he sped with the ball in one hand, blowing kisses with the other, and nailed him good and hard well short of the line. There were no more kisses, blown or otherwise, after that.

I met Tom Riddle, a small, wiry chap, at Kelso. It was, he said, his one big moment on the Rugby field. But he had something to remind him of it. Digging into a drawer, he produced a faded silk cap awarded to the Borderers who met the Maoris. He had also retained a programme from that far-off day. He chuckled when I told him the team-sheet would have been of little use to modern

Opening of the 1933 season at Earlston 'sevens' shows Selkirk slogging it out with Melrose.

spectators, let alone struggling reporters. The players were not numbered but were distinguished by the colour of the garters which held their stockings up. Tom's was purple. Not, I would imagine, of great help to a radio commentator in the fading light of a November day with the pitch a ploughed field.

CHAPTER THREE

Border Old Firms:
Hawick v Gala and the Rest

ONE characteristic common to all the Border towns and their Rugby clubs is that they have a guid conceit of themselves. They try not to make it sound like boasting, more an obvious statement of fact. Hawick, for instance, have been bragging in song and sentiment since time well-nigh immemorial that they are 'Queen o' a' the Borders'. Gala growl back that no other lads, least of all those of Hawick, 'can match the lads o' Gala Water'. Jed has always proclaimed to the confusion of potential enemies that 'Jethart's Here', whereupon they no doubt scattered. Selkirk, in its principal anthem, reveals its feelings for the eastern Borders by consigning that region 'tae the deil'. Even Langholm, who might seem a bit isolated for such squabbles over the garden fence, never fail to remind anyone within earshot that they inhabit, of course, 'the Muckle Toon'.

No wonder that on such fertile soil Border rivalries have acquired almost the patina of a religion. You doubt me? Why, it is not so long ago when Hawick were surprisingly beaten at Kelso, their first surrender to these opponents since national leagues began, and a state of something like mourning fell along the banks of the Teviot. Elders arrived for morning service at the historic St Mary's kirk next day, graver than usual and wearing black ties. Sensing the bereft state of the town and congregation, the

One of the great characters of Border Rugby, Doug Davies of Hawick. He was capped 20 times by Scotland in the 1920s, played (under the captaincy of Selkirk's Willie Bryce) for Scotland and Ireland against England and Wales in the Rugby Centenary Match, and figured in four Tests for the British Lions in South Africa in 1924.

minister began the service with a minute's silence. Everyone knew what for.

Where else, I wonder, would such a sense of communal grief following a Rugby reverse have found expression in the pews? Would the chapelgoers of Wales have sought divine guidance for troubled selectors? Rugby is, and always was, a serious business in the Borders with undertones to which the native especially is tuned. A man may be haunted for the rest of his life by one disastrously slack pass or over-confident goal-kick which was held to determine the adverse flow of a game. I heard of one player who emigrated to New Zealand after squandering a 3-2 overlap in favour of a drop kick which missed by a mile. Life was no longer tenable at home after such a misdemeanour as that.

Hawick and Gala are never likely to be twinned towns, but despite the caustic verses which they customarily exchange I suspect that they retain a good regard for each other. They would never admit it, of course, but they sense that in each other they usually find worthy opponents. A kind of Rangers-Celtic syndrome perhaps.

Hawick have come out of their contests with so many more tangible rewards that it is remarkable that the old magic of a Hawick v Gala confrontation remains. Perhaps it is because Gala's successes down the years have been so rare that they are especially savoured, whereas to Hawick it can only seem when the worst happens that it ranks as a negation of natural justice.

It always seems a sort of denial of the accepted rules of chance that Hawick should have won the Border League fully five times as often as Gala although they have been playing for it over the same span of time and generally looking as if they must be the front runners. I remember in the early 1930s Gala were strongly fancied to gain an even rarer prize, the unoffical Scottish championship and the Border League in the same season. They took the Scottish title with only two defeats in a long season and with a finely balanced side fired by such characters as Jimmy Ferguson, Henry Polson and Doddy Wood. But these two defeats were enough to deny them the Border Cup. Both had been inflicted by Hawick.

It is something of a curiosity that although there have been a few play-offs to decide the Border League, not one has involved Hawick and Gala. There have been Hawick v Jed, Hawick v Kelso, Hawick v Melrose, Kelso v Jed, but never a grandstand finale between the 'Old Firm' to decide the Border League. Maybe such a fixture would have been more than flesh and blood could bear.

However, there was one play-off between the Greens and Maroons which generated more excitement in its preliminary phase than on the day, or rather night, itself. It settled the First Division championship of 1977. Started four years earlier, Hawick

Gala's first 'Braw Lad', Henry Polson, who led the town's first Gathering ride in 1930 and played for Scotland against England a little earlier in the year, which was no bad lift-off for a brand-new Border festival. Henry was one of the district's true all-rounders, a first-class swimmer, a fine opening bat and one of Scotland's water polo stars.

had already taken it under their wing in the same sort of protective care which they habitually extended to the Border League. Indeed after winning the first five titles Hawick allowed only Heriot's to get briefly in on their act before Gala stoked the bonfire of old Border rivalry by winning thrice in four years.

Gala might have thrown down the gauntlet rather earlier, for the league was theirs for the taking in 1977. But it was not to be. Few who were involved will easily forget the rich drama of that final League Saturday. In theory three clubs, Hawick, Gala and West, could have finished ahead. They were dead level on match points and it was all up to differentials.

All won on the very last afternoon but it was by how much they won that mattered. West, with a margin of only 10 points, were instantly discarded. I was at Netherdale watching Gala running in six tries against unexpectedly stubborn Highland opposition. However, it seemed that Gala were doing enough, especially when the ground bristled to a buzz over the hot-line from Hawick that Selkirk were leading at half-time at Mansfield by 19-7. Surely Gala could not fail to land the title now.

As so often in the Hawick-Gala saga the twist lay in the tail. Gala finished the day with a respectable win by 31-3 which all of Netherdale assumed would be more than enough. What they did not know as the telephone line broke down (or seized up) was that Hawick had run riot as only they can in a fantastic second half. They ran in nine tries to trail in their wake a seemingly impregnable Selkirk lead and to leave the differential points gap exactly tied.

What followed proved something of an anti-climax, except to the legion of Hawick supporters who jostled with the rather apprehensive Gala fans on the big night at Melrose. Gala made a controversial team selection and were heavily beaten by 15-3. Dropped goals by the arch conspirators in Hawick's midfield, Jim Renwick and Colin Telfer, were exactly what Gala had feared. To be fair, Gala were handicapped by an injury to Drew Whitehead before the game was well under way. Nevertheless it was Hawick's 35th win in 38 consecutive Hawick and Gala games. Which, a follower of the Rev. Robert Dye might piously have claimed, was just about par for the course.

CHAPTER FOUR

The 'Big' Games: Days of Decision

NOWADAYS nothing stirs the blood in the Borders quite so much as a 'big' game, preferably against one of the leading overseas sides. Such fixtures come along at almost embarrassingly frequent intervals but there was a time when a generation might go by between one 'big' game and the next. Similarly, while there was the long break with France and the gaps between tours, it was much more difficult to build up an aggregate in caps. This explains why records which stood proudly to the credit of such kenspeckle Borderers as Doug Davies or Jock Beattie of Hawick, and seemed unassailable at the time, were overtaken and left far behind. How many caps would they have collected had they been born a generation or two later?

Next to gaining a cap, a game against an overseas side was always the supreme prize for Border players. They were hard to come by in the formative years. Between the original Maoris and the full-blown All Blacks there was a lapse of almost half-a-century and it was 20 years before they came again. No wonder those who had reached this eminence in a Rugby career and gone no further were remembered for it.

There were no claimants to even modest success, however, in the early matches, that first crack at the Maoris excepted. Border ambitions were badly dented by the South Africans of 1906 who ran rampant at Mansfield and won by 32-5. A long interval, and a world war, provided ample time for wounds to be licked before

15

the next onslaught from Down Under. This time it was a team rejoicing in a name which might not be instantly recognisable nowadays. They were not the Wallabies but the Waratahs, drawn not from all over Australia but only from the State of New South Wales and they dealt out an even more crushing blow to Border pride, winning by 36-nil.

Results of such severity would have been debilitating enough at any time, yet the curious fact is that they were absorbed at a time when Rugby prestige in the Borders was riding high. The first Springbok tour, for instance, coincided with an era when Jed-forest were Scotland's champion club and had contributed no fewer than 10 of the 30 players called to the international trial. It was much the same when the Waratahs cut their swathe through Border farmlands. Hawick were in the middle of a title-winning streak and Gala and Kelso were reckoned two of the best club teams in the country. The South XV for the New South Wales game included such justly renowned players as Jimmy Graham and R.T. Smith (Kelso), Willie Welsh and Rab Storrie (Hawick), John Goodfellow (Langholm) and Jimmy Ferguson and Doddy Wood (Gala). They were captained by the redoubtable David McMyn, a London Scottish cap who qualified through a Dumfries connection. Yet down they went under a barrowload of tries — tries, moreover, worth only three points in those days.

With all this as a backdrop to the next 'big' match, the arrival of the 1931 Springboks, and the undoubted impression that the Borders was currently caught in something of a trough, it was not to be wondered at that a then record crowd, estimated at 12,000, filled the Greenyards. How many of them saw the match I cannot say because the embankment was not all that steeply pitched. Once into the ground, however, it proved a game never to be forgotten. In my own case it was the first 'big' game I had been called upon to cover and my meagre stock of superlatives all but ran out.

The South XV contained all the expected names. They were captained by a richly experienced Hawick forward W.B. Welsh, who took clubmates Beattie and Foster into the pack with him. Graham, Wood, Aitchison and Polson were other names to conjure with but at the end of the day it was players with less

Jock Beattie (Hawick), one of the celebrated Teri triumvirate (the others were Welsh and Foster) who played for Scotland in the early 1930s. Beattie was rewarded with 23 caps and led his country in his final match at Twickenham. Best remembered with sleeves rolled, eyes aflame, exhorting his troops to play out of their skins. He put the wind up a Hawick newcomer in the Langholm dressing room by solemnly warning him that 'There's thoosands o' them oot there, and they're a' looking for you!'

claim to greater fame whose performance was imprinted on the memory.

The South Africans were a magnificently athletic side. By the time they arrived in Melrose their fame had gone ahead. They had swept all before them on a dazzling tour and one wondered if anybody could hold, let alone beat them. They paid South the compliment of fielding their 'Saturday' side. They had the bearing of supermen, bronzed with suntan from the veldt, formidably fit, aristocratic in green and gold. The South looked pygmies by comparison, small, squat, unsmiling with a rustic demeanour that may have misled the tourists over what was to come. At any rate it appeared to surprise them as much as it ignited the Border crowd when the South tore in and fairly rummled them up.

The Springboks were led by their taciturn captain, Bennie Osler, a stand-off of immense kicking power in an age when an ability to plonk the ball into the corner from within or without the 25-yard zone was just about all that mattered. He could also release his long leggy threequarters when he felt the moment was ripe and Osler was a player whose judgment or timing were hardly ever at fault. Something, however, went wrong with the precision mechanism, as Osler ruefully confessed afterwards, even if he was not sure exactly what.

I think I could tell him where his calculations miscarried. He had not allowed for the intensity of the Border tackling. Once the South started knocking their men down, the realisation grew that maybe the Springboks were not men from Mars after all. The more the South Africans came at them, the more they were thrown back. I suppose it must have felt a bit like ocean rollers breaking on the Cape coast. They were always driven back. It turned out to be a no-scoring draw, the only game of a long tour in which the South Africans failed to score, and that after beating all the four Home countries.

For years afterwards there were those who had stood in the crowd where they were best able to judge and swore that a refereeing aberration had perhaps cost the South an even more historic result. There were no television cameras then for a re-run and perhaps it was just as well. Late on in a game which must have been totally frustrating for the tourists the Borderers got the break they deserved. A pass in the Springbok midfield went adrift. Baillie, the Gala stand-off, got a foot to it. They could dribble the ball then and Baillie, controlling the ball beautifully, took off on a dribbling run almost up to the Springbok line. Brand, a legendary full back, who had possibly never seen anything quite like this before, came out to meet him like a goalkeeper cutting down the angle. Brand misjudged his dive, Baillie flicked the ball into the left corner and the ground shook to the roar as the rotund Melrose wing, Billy Nisbet, sped in on the ball and touched it down. It looked a good enough try, but no, said the referee, Malcolm Allan, who judged that Nisbet was fractionally ahead of Baillie as he pushed his shot into the corner. 'Ah well,' said a Melrose official afterwards, 'it was a good try' . . . and I know what he meant.

I suppose what I remember most about a game that was teeming with incidents of all kinds and provided a sensational result was the crack of doom quality of the tackling. Nothing else would have kept the enormously gifted Springboks out. One such tackle was delivered by Tommy Aitchison, the Gala full back, operating at centre, who caught Waring, a high-scoring centre, just as he was pressing on the accelerator and streaming for the line. It saved a certain five points. The other — I can see it yet — was even more bone-shaking. White, fast, leggy, was released around halfway in an uncluttered field. He seemed bound to score with no one to beat but the hunched, glowering 'Elky' Clark, Hawick's full back. What happened next I have never really been able to explain. It might have been a throw-back to the original Maoris match when a tourist had the cheek to blow a kiss. I'm sure White did not do anything so provocative as that but he was hit just the same by a tackle which echoed round the ground like a pistol shot. It saved the match. It convinced the Springboks that this was not their day. It was the perfect illustration of the old Scots maxim, 'wha daur meddle wi' me!'

CHAPTER FIVE

Border Favourites: Everybody Has Them

ANY Rugby fan rifling through his memories will find himself drawn inescapably to a line of demarcation between his 'great' players and his 'favourites'. They need not be the same. Talent and likeability do not always run in tandem, though as a rule they do. Although they were a bit before my time, I feel I must have missed a couple of real characters in Hawick's legendary Mattha Elliot and Davie Patterson. They played as quarter-backs in the 1890s and would have been classed as scrum-half and stand-off today, though they regarded these positions as interchangeable.

The argument over whether half-backs should be slotted into their pigeon-holes rumbled along for years, very much as later generations were to dispute the rival merits of a 3-2-3 and 3-4-1 scrum formation. No doubt it was like that when the early 20-a-side game was trimmed down to 15-a-side. Wherever did the redundant five go, for there was no replacement bench then?

Veteran Hawick supporters used to tell with relish of the shameless guile of Mattha and Davie, 'the best quarter-backs of their day' by general consent, certainly within range of Mansfield. Mattha, taciturn, calculating in attack, lethal in the tackle, must have complemented the contrasting skills of Davie, an imp of a man who was generally up to something. It was an endless source of indignation to Border followers of their fortunes that although both played for Scotland with distinction, their talents were never harnessed together in their country's cause. Club partnerships of

Hawick have had many great sides. Some would argue this was one of the best. They were Scottish and Border champions in 1926-27. *Standing (left to right)* R. Foster, R. Irvine, A. C. Pinder, J. B. Stevenson, R. N. Storrie, W. A. MacTaggart, J. Beattie. *Sitting* W. E. Anderson, J. Fraser, T. Glendinning, G. R. Cairns (Capt.), W. B. Welsh, C. H. Farmer, D. S. Davies. *In front* W. Corbett, C. Keillor.

this rare quality surface so seldom that one can only wonder at the purblind ways of selectors — then and now!

If the redoubtable Mattha and Davie never came under press-box scrutiny in my time (though Davie is still remembered in the Patterson Cup at Hawick 'sevens'), I did have the great good fortune to cover some of the later cantrips of their lineal descendants, Rab Storrie and Andra Bowie. They never merited serious consideration for a cap, but what entertainers they were! They must have been one of the slowest half-back pairs in Hawick's history, but what they lacked in pace about the paddock they more than made up for in their speed of thought and their telepathic communication. To see them at their best one had to attend a Border 'sevens' tournament, for it was in the shortened game that their talents truly blossomed. In those days the laws permitted more barefaced cheek than would be tolerated now, which suited Bowie and Storrie down to the ground. I have watched Bowie tee up a difficult penalty kick from close to touch, and take enormous care in sighting the posts, while the opposing side lined up in front of the bar on the off-chance of fortuitous possession. That was what Andra wanted them to think. Instead of going for goal he tapped the ball towards the corner flag and trundled up behind it unopposed for the sort of try for which even he managed to look apologetic.

Another favourite ploy was to break away from a scrum at close range as if in possession. The ball was left behind, tucked at the feet of the forwards, so that it was Storrie, in a hark-back to the old quarter-back days, who picked up and darted in for a score. Bowie's dummy was something quite special. Only the legendary G.P.S. Macpherson, in my experience, shared the same conjuror's knack of making the ball disappear. Bowie could hypnotise opponents into believing that the ball had been despatched on its way whereas it was still securely in his possession. No matter how regularly they were warned, defences still fell for it, even Border sides who ought to have known better. It was probably something to do with his bland, innocent mien as he padded surreptitiously through the gap.

Bowie became as solid a bulwark to the Hawick club after his playing days were done, his collection of 'sevens' medals reaching by then the staggering total of 54. Andra became one of the soundest of referees, a case, he used to comment, of poacher turning gamekeeper. He should know! He had tried all the dodges on the field. It was a notable tribute to his standing as a referee that when the official failed to arrive for one of Hawick's great New Year matches with Heriot's, then the biggest event in Scottish Rugby other than an international, the city side had no

---

Evergreen — in more ways than one! Jim Renwick, the Hawick centre who became Scotland's most capped back, enjoyed an international career spanning 11 seasons. Then he slipped back to his old junior club, Hawick Harlequins, to pass on the skills he had honed over the years while still emerging to play in some outlandish parts of the world (Saudi-Arabia, Sweden) alongside such old rivals as Mike Gibson (Ireland). Here he leads out the President's XV against the KOSB at Melrose in 1989. Renwick's wisecracks have a saltiness all their own. Once he watched Bruce Hay, never the speediest of Scottish full backs, trundle the length of the field and score. 'Well,' said Jim as Hay came back, 'I never thought I'd see it in slow-motion first time round!'

hesitation in accepting Bowie to handle the game, which he did with his usual good humour and scrupulous fairness. Bowie was one of the best judges I have known of young talent, and it was a well-deserved honour when he went as assistant manager of the Scottish Border Club (the South by their other name) 1960s tour in South Africa, a happy tour, incidentally, without any unwelcome political overtones.

Another player who struck me as larger than life both then and now was Gala's gangling Peter Brown ('P.C.' to the Rugby world). He was one of the celebrated Broons frae Troon and still loves to tell the story of how his brother Gordon phoned to ask if he had heard if a Scottish XV was chosen. It was and Peter gleefully announced that he was in. 'Who's out?' asked Gordon. 'You are!' Peter set up one record which, so far as I know, has not been challenged. He led his Scottish troops to victory over the auld enemy, England, on two successive Saturdays. It was 16-15 for the Calcutta Cup at Twickenham and 26-6 in the Centenary international at Murrayfield a week later.

I remember my old friend and colleague Jock Wemyss nudging me in a press-box to study the unconventional antics of one of the forwards. It was of course 'P.C.' who did not stand thoughtfully sucking his orange as his team-mates did but prowled round the circle of players like a caged lion waiting to burst out. Peter was an outstanding tearaway forward in his own right but I'm sure he'll be mainly remembered for his eccentric goal-kicking. It defied the laws of aerodynamics. The ritual never varied — plonk the ball on the deck, take a squint at the posts, wipe your nose, turn your back, wheel round and — wham! By the time Peter got his head up the ball was wobbling on an uncertain flight path to the posts. Usually it just limped over, sometimes with the odd ricochet. Peter once told me that he enjoyed giving them heart failure in the stand. It was fun for him — and rather nervous fun for us.

Of all the genial jokers in the Border Rugby pack there can be little doubt that George Stevenson of Hawick provided more merriment than most. 'Stevie' had the happy knack of making his most guileless afterthought seem like a preconceived plan. Most people of his generation will have seen him try a dropped goal — he was an inveterate optimist — from some unlikely location

One of the other 'Broons'. 'Big' Peter moved from West to Gala in the late 1960s and wound up with a bucketful of 28 caps and the unique distinction of captaining a winning Scotland XV against England twice in the same week. This was in the Calcutta Cup match of 1971 followed by the Centenary International at Murrayfield.

around midfield. The ball, often as not, would fly off the side of his foot and find a priceless touch right in the corner. If 'Stevie' had been trying for that touch he would probably have dropped a goal. 'Stevie' was an unlikely captain, with discipline and predictability never his strongest suits, but he had a way with him of getting results. I remember seeing him call correctly for Hawick at Inverleith one dense January day in the '60s. The fog lay so thick that from the midfield tunnel one could vaguely discern goalposts at one end of the ground and nothing at the other. 'Stevie' held up a finger to test the imaginary wind. 'Demm, it's

A quintet of Hawick caps proudly display their headgear in 1961. Back — G. D. Stevenson, T. O. Grant, A. Robson; front — J. J. Hegarty, Tom Wright (pres), H. F. McLeod.

blawing in circles.' Finally, after long deliberation and soul-searching, he bamboozled opposing captain and referee alike by declaring that 'We'll juist play wi' the fog'.

Not for nothing is he remembered as 'back-door Stevie'. He gained his first cap from a late call without even playing a trial. The selectors knew what they were about and he repaid them with a fine debut try. The interception was 'Stevie's' speciality — fine when it worked, disastrous when it didn't. He showed a cavalier attitude to the game. I'm not sure that he would have cared for the grinding seriousness of latter-day leagues. After that spectacular first cap somebody asked him if he would now be going for more. 'What's the point?' he joked. 'They tell me they're a' the same.' Same or not, Stevenson was to collect 24, sometimes by direct entry, sometimes via the back door, but he always gave abundant value in entertainment and very often in classy Rugby too.

Melrose came up with a player in Charlie Drummond who had a similarly unfettered attitude to the game. There was always a buzz when he got his fingers to a ball because one never quite knew what would happen next. Quite likely he would shoot off in a marvellously balanced piece of running, leaving man after man in his wake until the ball was planted over the try-line. He was only 16 when he played his first game for Melrose, having been discovered in nearby St Boswells. Had there been no Second World War Charlie would surely have become one of the most capped Border backs. As it was, he had to await demob before he could pull on a Scottish jersey in a full-blown international though he did figure in two of the 'victory' games. Charlie picked up 11 caps over the next four seasons but one sometimes sensed that his heart was not entirely in Rugby, not at least when there was a good 'run' on the river. His other passion was fishing. Melrose could never be entirely sure of his availability when the fish were moving. Rugby, of course, won in the end and he went on to lead Melrose to their first unofficial championship in the early '50s and to give great service to the game as a selector, overseas tour manager and S.R.U. President. All that with the odd trout fly in his pocket.

CHAPTER SIX

The High Flyers: Borderers Who Set the Pace

I FORGET who it was who said that it was harder to get into the Scottish XV than out, probably the same chap who swore the selectors gathered in a huddle behind the old clubroom at Earlston on the first day of the season and sketched out the international side. The sprinkling through the records of 'one cap wonders' disproves this theory but it does seem that once selectors become convinced of the high degree of commitment, temperament and technique of a player they are reluctant to let him go, especially if he fits in well with the social life of the squad.

The Borders has produced a wildly disproportionate number of these favourite sons, whose inclusion in the national side over many years was never challenged. Indeed, the first dozen names of all-time 'greats' in the current Scottish roll of fame contains seven Borderers, all of them home-produced. There have been a few high flyers over the years who came to the district in search of a first cap and, having got it, flew off again. I would not include them in this chapter, but the high incidence of true Borderers from just seven senior clubs must be something of a reproach to the rest of Rugby Scotland.

Unlikely to be challenged for some time, if at all, as their country's most experienced caps are Jim Renwick and Colin Deans. Neither played Rugby outside his native Hawick and they accumulated 52 caps apiece. Not only that but when they retired they had established a world record in their positions, centre and

Durable 'twins', John Rutherford (Selkirk) and Roy Laidlaw (Jed) who set up a world-record partnership at half-back in the 1980s. Here they are in action with the South.

hooker respectively. Both gave me endless pleasure throughout their long careers in the 1970s and '80s, not just because they were such peerless technicians but because they possessed that touch of individuality which could light up the dullest game.

Renwick always looked older than he was. A receding hairline even in his apprentice days gave him something of the air of a veteran and his command of the midfield reflected it. If he ever felt tension, and it could not have been often, it was relieved by a mannerism which became known throughout the district. He slapped his palms on a bald pate and pulled them down over his eyebrows. What kind of therapy that was I am not sure but it certainly did the trick with Jim. I remember him following the procedure as his boot struck the ball in an injury-time penalty against Gala, no ordinary local derby either, but a decider for the

From down on the farm, the three Cranston brothers, David, Alistair and Ian, who made a powerful contribution to Hawick's fortunes in the 1970s. Alistair won 10 caps, mainly alongside his favourite foil, clubmate Jim Renwick.

Division One championship. Most of Renwick's team-mates could not bear to look and simply turned their backs on the 45-yard kick as if it was nothing to do with them. Many of the Gala side found something to distract them on the distant horizon. Renwick, however, just kicked the goal.

Apart from the impression of studied calm and barely suppressed mischief, Renwick had one trump card to bemuse his opponents and, indeed, the referee. He was a master of the Hawick dialect. No need for a code where Jim was concerned provided the other player was a Hawick man too. A visiting referee once enquired if he was Welsh. 'No, but yon chap in the stand', with a sweep towards the distant figure of the old British Lion, Willie Welsh, 'hey is!' Jim gained one of his 52 caps as a replacement wing. His regular colleague of nearly 300 sorties with Hawick, Alistair Cranston, was already out in midfield. As Jim passed him to take up station he called out, 'Hey, Alistair, whit dae ah dae oot here?'

Renwick missed out on many of the accolades showered on his contemporaries, possibly, I suspect, because he was so reluctant to

Where's the ball? Colin Deans (Hawick), who set a world record as an international hooker, was never one to bury his head in a scrum for too long. Here he cocks an eye at things for South against Japan in 1986.

give up as a player. He carried on well into his mid thirties with his original Hawick junior club. How many Rugby celebrities would have done that? Mind you, he did emerge from time to time to team up with some of his old contemporaries such as Mike Gibson of Ireland in taking Rugby to such improbable venues as Sweden and Saudi Arabia, nor did he duck the odd showpiece game in Northern Ireland. Renwick will be remembered not only as a great player but as a great amateur.

Deans, perhaps, conveyed a greater air of authority and dedication. He was a hooker who hated to lose a strike or a game, a front-row specialist who never accepted that he could not take the field as effectively as the average back and who had the wit and pace to stay with a movement no matter where it went. He kept turning up in some extraordinary places. Most of all Deans was a demanding leader. He did not suffer slackers or fools gladly. He demanded results and usually got them in a thoroughly pleasant way. Perhaps the oddest feature of Deans' early years is that he never made it to the Hawick High School 1st Year XV. Somebody told him he was too fat so he went off and played soccer. His father hooked for Hawick in a championship-winning side of the 1940s, so lurking talent eventually came out and turned Deans in double quick time into one of the finest hookers in the trade. He was at the acme of his powers when he hooked for Scotland in the Grand Slam of 1984.

If there was any deep disappointment in his career, it can only have been his failure to oust Ciaran Fitzgerald from the hooker's berth on the British Lions tour of New Zealand in 1983. The Irishman, of course, was captain, which just shows how important it is at any level to choose a skipper who can command his place. Deans made a speciality of accurate, often well disguised, throwing in from touch. Fitzgerald was hopeless at it. The Lions management failed to perceive the error of their ways but Deans was entitled to a rueful grin the following year when he helped Scotland to clinch the Triple Crown at Lansdowne Road while his arch-rival, cast out of the Irish team, watched glumly from the stand.

Just behind this illustrious Hawick pair in the international placings is their less ebullient colleague, Alan Tomes, who crept up towards the half-century in appearances for Scotland, setting his own record for the position of lock and never showing less than total commitment. I have always felt that Tomes deserved a special award to recognise the number of times he crossed and re-crossed the old frontier to play and train at Hawick. Despite an impeccable Teviotdale background (his father captained a Hawick junior club) Tomes was brought up on Tyneside and could readily have staked out a Rugby career in the North-East of England. That option was quickly rejected and he became a fixture in the Greens for nearly two decades. A crafty line-out specialist and teak-like lock, he was, I suppose, one of the best 'rummlers-up' of his day.

Hawick have not by any means claimed a monopoly of the pace-setters in caps. Keith Robertson is now the most capped Melrose player but his career has taken off time and again after some critics had laid it to rest. With over 40 international appearances

When Arthur Brown was picked as Scotland's full back in 1972 he needed no introduction to five of the team. Like him they were all Gala players. Arthur, the 'wee Broon' of Gala's triumvirate from the clan, was one of the lethal goal-kickers of his day. In addition to playing on five occasions for his country he had the rare distinction of being chosen as Scotland-Ireland's full back against England-Wales.

the selectors kept turning to him as a player who might revitalise the Scottish midfield and they were not disappointed. Robertson was always one of the best-balanced runners in the land with a quickness of vision and mind to match.

Two of the district's smaller club, Jedforest and Selkirk, have between them produced the most durable half-back partnership in Roy Laidlaw and John Rutherford. That selectors regarded them as inseparable in the key positions which often invite experiment shows just how good they were. They were at their commanding best in the 1984 Grand Slam year and it was sheer disaster that their mesmeric collaboration could not be carried forward into the first World Cup. As so often happens, when one half of a duo goes some of the magic goes too. They will be recalled with Eck Hastie and David Chisholm, the Melrose and Scotland half-backs of a couple of decades earlier, as among Rugby's aristocrats.

Perhaps Gala cannot match Hawick in lofty statistics of the kind I have quoted but one wonders what kind of totals Arthur Brown and Peter Dods might have set had their birth dates not fallen on either side of Andy Irvine, who reigned supreme at full back for ten eventful years. Brown was one of the six Gala players — the others were Peter Brown, John Frame, Jock Turner, Duncan Paterson and Nairn McEwan — who set one highly cherished record by facing England on the same day, and winning. Arthur, 'the wee Broon' to his countless admirers, had much the same style as Peter Dods. He was small, compact, unexpectedly fast, able to break off either foot, and absolutely fearless under the high ball, no matter how many opposing hooves were clattering in his ears. Both could also kick goals. Irvine supplanted Brown just when he was getting into his international stride. Dods had a much longer initial spell of 16 games

Two of Melrose's favourite sons, Keith Robertson and Craig Chalmers, in their first game together for the South in 1987. Robertson retired from the international scene two years later, just as Chalmers was picking up his first cap. Robertson can claim one headstart on his young colleague — 14 years earlier at the outstart of his career and when only 20, he won the Rugby souvenir that probably means most of all to a Melrose player — a Melrose 'sevens' medal.

before he was challenged by the flamboyant Watsonian, Gavin Hastings. He might well have receded into the shadows, satisfied with a tidy haul of caps and a Grand Slam. But not Peter. Typically his appetite for the game remained as voracious as ever, as he sat on the bench in game after game watching Hastings hog the headlines. When Hastings eventually fell victim to injury there was never the slightest doubt who would take his place, and when that happens to a player who has been out of the side for four seasons I suspect it is a special kind of tribute.

Dods and Hastings were both selected for the 1989 Lions in Australia. This time the pendulum swung the other way. Hastings was chosen for the first Test, and although it miscarried for the Lions he played well enough to hold his place. Two Test wins to clinch a famous tour followed and finally a game against the combined Australia-New Zealand side. How ironical that over the tour Dods and Hastings shared the highest points total — 66 apiece.

CHAPTER SEVEN

Pinged on the Wing:
They Never Made it to Murrayfield

EVERYONE feels instinctive sympathy for the player who gets so near and so far — and all because of no fault of his own. In Rugby, caps generally come along in the wake of years of application and sweat. Even when they come early, as a first cap did to Melrose's 20-year-old Craig Chalmers, it came via a long stepladder reaching down to a Border under-15 side up through the age groups, a 'B' game and a Scotland XV tour. How shattering, therefore, when everything seems guaranteed to take you all the way and the last rung breaks and you plummet to earth. I remember consoling one for whom this had been his fate. It could have been worse — he might have been a 'one-cap wonder'. Quite a number of those who advanced to the portals of fame are still fondly remembered while the others who just squeezed through are not.

No one in the Borders had more reason to rail against churlish fate than Hawick's flame-haired flanker of the early 1970s, Wat Davies. He was perpetual motion personified, first to the break of every ball, fearless in the tackle, a studious tactician. There was just one thing that bothered his host of admirers — he was undeniably 'wee'. He turned the scales at just over 12 stones and looked more like a centre than the prospective member of an international pack. His consistency on the field and his sheer flair

37

could not be denied and ultimately the Scottish selectors took a deep breath and chose him to play against Wales. Most new caps wrap themselves in cottonwool till the great day dawns. Not so Davies. He played for Hawick as usual on the Saturday before the international and sustained a serious knee injury which led to a cartilage operation. Nor was that all, for further illness and a stomach operation followed and he was obliged to retire from serious Rugby. There could not have been a more heartbroken young man unless it was the French forward who stormed up the tunnel at Stade Colombes on his way to his first cap — and broke an ankle. To Davies it must have seemed just like that.

Everybody who has watched Border Rugby over the years will have compiled a personal list of players who ought to have been capped but somehow weren't. Mine starts with a name a lot of folk may overlook, Bill McLaren. After returning from Army service in Italy in World War II Bill rapidly became a permanent member of a powerful Hawick pack. He was an obvious candidate for the top. I am positive he would have made it for he had all the attributes of a hungry Hawick forward, always on the ball, always looking to do something with it, always delivering his full weight in the scrum. Bill got as far as two international trials and was clearly destined to go further when, to the consternation of a host of friends, he contracted tuberculosis and spent two years in a sanitorium. That was the end of a dream but another one was realised, in a vicarious sort of way, when he became a radio and then a TV commentator and finally had the rare satisfaction of watching from the commentary box as his son-in-law Alan Lawson stepped out in a Scottish jersey.

One of my favourite candidates for the list of 'great uncappeds' is an old Langholm forward who might contest the case and brandish a copy of Hansard to prove me wrong. No one at Westminster ever believed that Sir Hector Monro, M.P. for Dumfriesshire, had not played for Scotland. If he hadn't, then he ought to have done, went the general argument. What confused the Honourable Members was that after a distinguished but in the ultimate analysis unrewarded playing career, Hector went on to an influential spell in the upper echelons of the game. He became an international selector, President of the S.R.U., even Minister

Recognise them? Hawick's Greens sported the kilt for their first post-war visit to London Scottish in 1949. Back (left to right) — H. Bouglas, E. A. Nixon, W. Reid, J. J. Hegarty; front — S. Coltman, P. Deans, J. Kennedy, H. Scott, J. R. McCredie, R. Sheriff, G. R. Hook, W. Fraser.

of Sport — so he must have played for Scotland, mustn't he? Of course he should. Those who remember Sir Hector in the days when he was a member of that fearsome Langolm 'sevens' triumvirate, Grieve, Telford and Monro, are still puzzling out why.

It's often a matter of another place, another time where international recognition is concerned. Some win a cap because there is no one else around, others are crowded out by the competition. Even so, and after many years, I am still mystified by the omission of two Melrose worthies who would have surely strolled into the side in any other era, and perhaps should have done in their own. Derek Brown was as honest and hard-working a forward as you would ever clap eyes on. He would have topped any popularity poll of Scottish forwards in his day. He played in the Melrose back row for 14 years, he made over 40 appearances for the South, he played twice against the Springboks and the Wallabies, he was invited into the select company of Barbarians, and he picked up some 35 'sevens' medals. His father, Bob, was the genial secretary at the Greenyards for many years and the whole family had deep roots in Melrose Rugby lore. Maybe now that he has himself been elevated to a seat on the S.R.U. committee he will get the chance to burrow through some musty minutes and find out just what they had against him. A lot of Border fans would have loved to know!

While he is at his researches Derek could also investigate the equally odd omission of his old colleague, Alastair Frater, the elegant centre who made so many of Charlie Drummond's tries. A few miles away at Netherdale one could alight on two dynamic forwards, Nat Carson and Johnny Gray, who were confidently expected to break through to Scottish ranks, but strangely never did. I always felt that their forthright contribution was more worthy of recognition than that of some who got the nod. Over at Hawick there was a rucking flanker, Graham Lyall, who looked tailor-made for a Scottish berth but who evidently didn't fit. Maybe he made a cardinal mistake in choosing to play for his beloved Hawick in an important club game when he had also been selected by the South. It is sometimes on such decisions that caps are gained and lost.

CHAPTER EIGHT

The Greatest Club Teams: Or Were They?

IN my very early days on the Border Rugby carousel I remember an old worthy — not a habitué of either Mansfield or Philiphaugh — staunchly declare that the best club team in Britain would be 'Hawick's forrits and Selkirk's backs'. I know what he meant. The Greens at that time, around the '20s, were a fearsome lot with Doug Davies driving them along in his imperious style and youngsters like Jock Beattie, Jerry Foster and Willie Welsh fast cottoning on. Selkirk supplied the subtlety which Hawick lacked. The influence of Willie Bryce lingered on and backs of the rich promise of Peter Reid, Heatlie Cockburn, Bertie Dodds and George Wilson were honing their skills. Unfortunately the theory could never be put to the test as in contests between the two it was almost invariably the formidable Hawick forwards who won.

In staking out one's belief that any club side was 'the greatest' there is bound to be a good deal of subjectivity in the judgment. Even more, one must try to assess what the opposition was like. It's one thing to knock off ten of the first 15 official championships, as Hawick did. That says a lot about the blend and balance of a well-organised side, but doesn't it also hint at the decline and fall of some of the big names of Scottish Rugby? The Greens could never hog the old unofficial championship like this. The 'newspaper' table had its imperfections but it was an acceptable if rough yardstick of consistency over a season. The title went to the team with the best percentage among upwards of

41

30 clubs who did not all play each other. Occasionally there was a wildcat result but for the most part clubs accepted it and enthusiasm could run high. It helped too that no one was relegated.

One thing to be said for the unofficial days: the favours were spread around remarkably well. Kelso, Selkirk, Melrose, Langholm and Jed were all able to claim the championship in post-war years before the official leagues were born. The title also went to city clubs who have all but sunk without trace. Jordanhill College, for instance, Allan Glen's, Hillhead, Royal High and Dunfermline were all able to lord it briefly over Border sides. This suggests that talent was more evenly spread and that perhaps in one's search for the 'greatest' club sides it might be as well to stray a bit beyond the tight confines of the official championship.

Gala will no doubt feel that the side which gained three First Division titles in four years in the early 1980s was as redoubtable as any they've ever had. They certainly tapped a rich reservoir of talent at this time, with such forwards as David Leslie, Jim Aitken, the Grand Slam skipper, and Tom Smith at the peak of their considerable powers. Yet for me Gala's single success in the unofficial table was something else. Back in 1932 one wondered if the Maroons, one of the oldest clubs in Scotland, would ever come into their own. Repeatedly the pickings somehow got away. They were the first Border club to have a player capped, they had regularly led the pack, but the ultimate prize kept eluding them. And how they hated being forever in the shadow of their great rivals, Hawick.

In one dramatic campaign Gala changed all that. They had a born leader in Jimmy Ferguson who had a fiery lieutenant in Henry Polson, the first 'Braw Lad' at the town's annual festival. The pack was glad to serve as purveyors to a back division of all the talents. Their eager running Rugby was pure joy. Calling the shots were their contrasting half-backs, Bobby Boyd, a scrum-half with a pandora's box of ploys, and the lanky, nonchalant Andrew Baillie who was a lot faster than he looked. In midfield were two of the most creative Border centres I have seen, Doddy Wood and Tommy Aitchison, carving out scores for pacey wings, Matheson and Barbour. Behind them lay the brooding presence of Bobby

A picture Kelso had long been awaiting. The full squad with Gary Callendar (captain) and Charlie Stewart (coach) who first brought the Scottish championship to Poynder Park in 1988.

Waddell, a full back not given to allowing an opponent to get anywhere near his line.

Gala made a flying start on what was to be their breakthrough season. In their first match they overcame Glasgow Accies, then one of the most accomplished sides in the land with such giants as Herbert Waddell, Max Simmers, Jimmy Nelson and Jimmy Dykes in their ranks. On this dramatic win Gala built a season of sustained quality. Scenes once familiar in Border towns were enacted when Gala returned by train from their final match at Jock's Lodge, having beaten Royal High and become custodians of a championship as ethereal as the Triple Crown. Real or not, Gala savoured it to the full. Half the town were there to welcome them from the train. Every member of the side was carried shoulder high to the Douglas Hotel. 'Hail the champs' became as much a Gala byword as 'Braw, Braw Lads'. The fact that it all happened around the time the local Gathering was being established certainly helped.

Celebrations were repeated a few weeks later when Gala won

Alan Tomes (Hawick), the most capped Scottish lock of his day, soars above Ken McLeish (Melrose) in a Border League match. Tomes could probably claim one more record, that of crossing the Cheviots more often than anyone else to play Rugby in Scotland. For over 17 years he travelled regularly to train and play at Hawick.

Peter Dods, who was Scotland's full back in the Grand Slam triumph of 1984, lost his place a year later to Gavin Hastings. He then sat patiently on the bench through 18 internationals until his chance came again and not only did he play in all the Five Nations games of 1989 but he went on to claim a place in the British Lions tour of Australia.

the Melrose Jubilee 'sevens'. There was only one cloud on the horizon. Gala had captured the unofficial championship with no more than two defeats. Alas, these two defeats were sustained at the hands of Hawick who thereby claimed the Border League Cup. What you might describe as a spectre at the feast, but it was still a time for feasting at Netherdale.

The unofficial table produced anomalies, which led to blazing rows, conducted in private of course as the Union did not recognise the championship anyway and no one would step out of line by even hinting that such a thing existed. The newspapers eventually sorted out which matches could be included and which rejected. Even so, Selkirk had a fortunate escape in their year of grace, 1953. No one foresaw what satisfaction that season could bring at Philiphaugh, least of all in the previous autumn when they somehow contrived to lose a holiday game to Allan Glen's by 13-12. Who cared? Nobody did until after the New Year when it dawned on Selkirk officials that they might have a chance of the unofficial championship. By now form horses were falling over the sticks and Selkirk kept plugging on. Margins were tight — 6-3 against Melrose, 3-3 against Langholm, 5-3 against Edinburgh Wanderers, 6-0 against Glasgow Accies, 3-0 against Gala, but they were still on course. They came to the final game, an evening fixture at Philiphaugh against Jed, needing only to win by however slim a margin to be hailed as 'champs'. What an 80 minutes of exquisite torture for home followers that proved to be! They clung desperately to the narrowest of leads, a Tom Brown dropped goal, for most of the game, nerves raw and the crowd pleading with them to hold out. Just as the referee had clearly decided to blow up on the next dead ball a huge drop emerged from Jed. It was triggered at halfway and it seemed to be on the right trajectory to bisect the posts until a providential wisp of wind crept down the valley and deflected the kick just outside the near post. The subsequent sound was not so much a cheer as of gas escaping from a punctured balloon. Still, it had been a great year for Selkirk and for their phlegmatic captain, George Downie, who with two internationalists, Jim Inglis and Jock King, controlled operations from the front row. An adventurous full back, Archie Little, who seemed well ahead of his time by

One of the features of post-war Border Rugby was the number of city players who winged their way South in search of higher honours. Nairn McEwan (Highland to Gala and back again) was one who found what he was seeking. The move worked out too for Iwan Tukalo, son of a Ukranian father and Italian mother, who made a switch from Royal High to Selkirk and was soon an international wing.

emerging so regularly from deep defence, ball in hand, added to the apprehensions which many Selkirk followers felt before the title was finally nailed down. Yet it was as well balanced a side as Selkirk have ever produced, a big rawboned pack and a set of backs who reckoned that a try saved was as good as a try scored. But, my, did they live dangerously!

Kelso demonstrated the same racy qualities three decades on when, after two seasons of getting so near and yet so far, they finally entered into their kingdom in 1988. It was a nerve-jangling business. Percentages were discarded with the unofficial championship and in a tie at the top it all depended on who had the better points differential. I was at Kelso for their final match with Heriot's. They were never seriously pressed and won by a comfortable 35-nil. No wild exultation at the final whistle, however, but rather a deafening calm as the wires crackled between Poynder Park and Mansfield and the Kelso president finally used the loudspeakers to announce 'For the first time in our history . . . ' Nobody heard the rest. Kelso had done it!

When the cheering stopped it was confirmed that Hawick had beaten Musselburgh by 51-3, which was not quite enough. Kelso were 31 points clear and that, to the chagrin of the Greens, meant that the title was on its way to Kelso. But at least it stayed in the Borders, as Hawick stressed in their generous congratulations — 'no' lost what a friend gets!' Kelso were popular champions. Not only did they lose just one league game (to Hawick, naturally), but they produced a brand of open Rugby which won a host of friends.

For Gary Callendar it was a day when dreams came true. Not only had he led Kelso to a famous triumph but in the same season he had taken over as Scotland's hooker from Colin Deans, and that after 23 weary afternoons on the bench. It must have seemed even a longer wait than his club endured. Kelso's success sprang in part from their brisk, brusque pack in which John Jeffrey and Eric Paxton deployed their contrasting skills to rare effect. Bob Hogarth and Andrew Ker were happily in tune at half-back, the threequarters were given a sharp cutting edge by Alan Tait and

Roger Baird, and behind them there lay the cavalier figure of Marshall Wright, a young full back just beginning to make his way in the game and showing any amount of flair. In short it was almost a pleasure to lose to such talented champions as Kelso but one has to add that they let the Border title slip to Jed by a single point in the play-off at Melrose. Odd how regularly accidents like that have happened over the years.

CHAPTER NINE

Crossing the Rubicon: Lure of Rugby League

THERE was a time when a Border Rugby player who went professional might as well have blasted off into outer space. His pals, or at least his club officials, never forgave him. I have known blokes come bouncing back to the Borders after playing Rugby League only to find that they were scarcely allowed inside their old ground. Willie Welsh, who won 21 caps and a Test place with the Lions while with Hawick, went over so late in his career that he could almost have retired. Getting a job back in hosiery, he did some Saturday afternoon reporting, but there was one threshold he never crossed, into his old Mansfield dressing room, after he had been warned off by a fussy official. An old Gala international half-back who went professional was even denied admission to a dance in support of Rugby funds.

It's hard nowadays to realise how deep lay the hostility between the two codes and how unforgiving many otherwise likeable Union officials were. Legalistically the position has barely changed but on a human scale relations have mellowed. Old players who have sampled life on the other side of the divide are no longer treated as pariahs. Yet once they did not even need to put pen to paper to incur Union sanctions. I can recall two admirable club players, one from Melrose, one from Hawick, who were booted out of amateur Rugby on suspicion that they had taken part in a trial for a professional club.

One can understand the bitterness of the era. After World War One the Northern Union, as Rugby League then was, could

Who would anticipate finding a Border Rugby star at Wembley? That's where George Fairbairn, former Kelso full back, finished up in the Rugby League Cup Final of 1986 instead of Twickenham. He went to Wigan as a professional at a time when Scotland seemed overstocked with class full backs and promptly gained the Test places he would almost certainly have won in the amateur game.

tempt an amateur player into their fold for as little as £200 and a £5 a week job. With slack times in hosiery and tweed mills, and possibly a girl friend eager to be married, the lure was for some well-nigh irresistible. Jed lost half-a-dozen of their best players in a single season. It was a particular blow when George Douglas, capped against Wales, went over the fence. His brother Jimmy, also surely a prospective Scottish cap, went the same way. Their father, incidentally, had been heavyweight professional wrestling champion of the world, which might well have conditioned them to what lay ahead in the unarmed combat of what was then a thoroughly pugilistic Rugby League. Years later I met Jimmy who by now had rounded off his career as manager of Oldham, the only Borderer, so far as I know, to reach this rung on the professional ladder. He told me that, like so many more who went

over, the decision was dictated by the harsh financial facts of the
times. Even a few hundred pounds was a fortune when you were
out of work. Willie Welsh was probably the most richly experienced player ever recruited from the Borders. Most of the
others were at the outset of their careers. Welsh went for £800. His
clubmate Alex Fiddes, perhaps as fine a prospect as Scotland ever
had at stand-off but as yet uncapped, went for a paltry £300.

One of the factors which fuelled the hostility between the two
codes was the fear that professional Rugby might somehow gain a
footing in the Borders. In nearly a century it has come no nearer
than Carlisle though I cherish among a clutch of bizarre memories
a ladies 13-a-side match laid on for demonstration purposes at, of
all places, the little Roxburgh village of Ancrum. Some of my
journalistic colleagues wondered, enviously, what it had been like
in the changing room. All I could tell them was that the props
seemed more pleasingly moulded. As for the rest I couldn't see for
the steam! There was a brief flirtation with Rugby League in
Glasgow in the '50s where the Stepps stadium was earmarked for a
Second Division side to be known as the Black Eagles, Alas, the
Eagles, so far as I know, never left the nest.

Since the Second World War what was once a spate has
dwindled to a trickle. Few Borderers have gone over, a reflection
of changing social mores, a more flexible stance by Union chiefs,
and, dare one say it, the quiet realisation that rewards might be
quite as agreeable in the one code as the other. One of my first
post-war assignments involved a journey through what for me was
alien country to Swinton in Lancashire. I was despatched to cover
the deciding Great Britain v Australia Test. The sole interest so
far as I was concerned lay in the appearance of Tom McKinney
and Dave Valentine from Jed and Hawick respectively. Not many
Borderers have got as far as a Test place in Rugby League where,
of course, opportunities are thinner on the ground. No Five
Nations, for instance, and just the odd overseas side or France.

One hears plenty about Borderers who made good in Rugby
League but little about those who just gently faded away — and
there have been plenty of them. Some probably were too hasty in
accepting the first offer which was dangled before them. They
should have examined not just what was offered but who was

Rugby League's most spectacular capture from the Borders in many years was Alan Tait, the Kelso international centre, in 1988. He was a competitive player, likely to hold his place in any Scottish XV for years to come. Widnes got a bargain. They converted him from centre to full back and in next to no time he was in the Great Britain side to face France.

making it. Two of the genuine success stories both come from the same position, full back, and the same Border club, Kelso. George Fairbairn looked a certainty to make the Scottish XV in one position or another when, at 20, he decided to head south. One of the things which made up his mind was that Andy Irvine had emerged as a world-class full back who was unlikely to be dislodged from the Scottish XV for many years to come. In fact, he was there for a decade. Oddly it was Irvine who was partly responsible for Fairbairn's move. He was regularly approached by men with fat cigars and fatter cheque books but Irvine's loyalty to Rugby Union was absolute. In desperation one of the scouts asked him who was the next best full back in Scotland. 'Oh, it's George Fairbairn, of course', and with that Wigan were hotfoot to Kelso and one of the most profitable signings they have ever made.

Fairbairn had star quality. In no time he was in the England then the Great Britain teams.

Even swifter recognition came the way of Alan Tait who made eight appearances in a Scottish jersey, helped to propel Kelso towards their first Scottish championship, and then accepted a massive offer from Widnes. His fee was that which had tempted Willie Welsh all those years before — with a couple of noughts added. The weekly wage was also an improvement! Widnes lost no time in turning Tait from a centre into a full back. In the professional game the requirements are much the same. Despite fierce competition Tait fought his way into two games for Great Britain against France in his first season, an ascent to fame which left certain former Welsh stars looking somewhat aghast. It's nice to add that, in changing times, Fairbairn and Tait could go back to Kelso, share a crack and a drink with their old buddies — but not, such are the heavily manned frontiers of the two codes, a friendly game of Rugby.

CHAPTER TEN

Border Gift to Rugby: Nothing like The 'Sevens'

IF it were not for the thought that a rich diet of cream puffs and champagne is not to be recommended, I would wager that a fair number of Border folk honestly believe we should have been playing 'sevens' all along. So much for the importunate Rugby schoolboy who picked up the ball and ran with it. If he had waited fifty years Ned Haig, a Melrose man, might have shown him how to do it!

In its way the emergence of the seven-a-side game at the Greenyards was no accident, whereas that celebrated Webb Ellis improvisation certainly was. Ned was casting around for a fund-raising idea when he hit upon the notion of a knock-out miniature Rugby tournament worked into an afternoon of athletic sports. Haig, who was originally from Jedburgh, could not have guessed what he had begun. 'Sevens' were an instant success on their home patch. Within two years Gala (1884) and Hawick (1885) had launched their own competitions on similar lines. Before long every club in the district made the startling discovery that it was possible to raise as much revenue on a single 'sevens' afternoon as, very likely, in an entire fifteen-a-side campaign, and to delight their supporters into the bargain.

Money, of course, was crucially important. No sponsors then to lavish largesse on amateur sports clubs in return for free publicity and hospitality tents. If teams wanted to improve their changing

The Langholm seven who recorded their first success at Hawick in 1899.
Centre (with ball) is Tom Scott, who was the club's first cap. Front right is
David Elliott, great-uncle of Tommy Elliott, a 1970s cap. David Elliot could
claim one odd record — he was a reserve for Scotland and England on the same
day. This came about because he sometimes played for his home town,
Langholm, and sometimes for Carlisle, where he worked. Both countries
fancied him!

facilities, put up a stand or simply swell the 'kitty', then 'sevens'
was the way to do it.

By April the fifteen-a-side card was virtually finished anyway
and cricket had barely begun. Crowds flocked to the sword-play
of 'sevens'. Moreover a field populated by only 14 players instead
of the normal 30 created scope for all manner of ploys. Club
games tended to heavy frontal assault, with packs heaving and
grunting at each other, backs always mindful of the tactical touch

Fifty years on and Langholm do it again. They registered their second 'sevens' success at Selkirk in 1949. Back (left to right) — Alex Woodhouse, John Waldie, Jim Grieve, Jim Telford; front, Donald Scott, Hector (now Sir Hector) Monro and Jim Maxwell. A year later Langholm had their third success at Gala in the most economical way possible, their aggregate throughout the day being just four scores to one.

kick, and full backs, hardly ever, apart from the most irrational, venturing forth from last-ditch defence. Players were like whippets let off the leash. This liberated form of Rugby became compulsive watching. There were other things, too. The seven-a-side tournaments became great meeting places in a way that Murray-field and the other big grounds were later to become. One heard the rich dialects of all the Border towns. With luck one could identify some, perhaps even understand the odd phrase, in between sampling the hot pies, the lemonade lorry and the horse-drawn 'chipper'. A more civilised way of spending a sunny April afternoon no Borderer could imagine.

It took an unconscionable time for the Border invention of shortened Rugby to penetrate the rest of the sporting world, though there can hardly be a country left to conquer now. Maybe the cities felt they could not reproduce the couthy ambience of

A strong contender for the claim to be the best Border seven of all time. Hawick's team of 1927 which won all five Border trophies in succession. Back (left to right) — W. A. Mactaggart, A. C. Pinder, Andra Bowie, Rab Storrie; front — J. Fraser, G. R. Cairns, D. Patterson (pres), D. S. Davies, W. B. Welsh.

the Border grounds. In that they were probably correct as the chequered career of Edinburgh's 'Infirmary Sevens' was eventually to prove. By the early 1920s — 40 years after Ned Haig had dreamed his dream — 'sevens' stormed the very bastion of the English establishment and the Twickenham tournament was born.

It is worth noting, however, that the Rugby Union was not in close contact with its far-flung outposts and apparently hadn't heard that Tynedale, in north Northumberland, had appeared at the very first Melrose 'sevens' and were good enough to win at Gala and Hawick in 1885 and at the Greenyards in 1886. The penetration slowly spread to the broad waters of the Tyne and it seemed wholly fitting that the first Scottish winners of an English tournament in 1920 should be a Border club, Selkirk. By now 'sevens' was making converts everywhere. Melrose themselves have had among their guests the American Cougars, the French Barbarians, Hong Kong and Racing Club de Paris. Jed have numbered Argentinians among their guests while Canadians have tried their luck at Selkirk. A Scottish Border seven has reached

Few players can have retired so young as 33 and gone straight to a seat on the South selectors. This was Colin Telfer's experience. He won 17 caps as a thoughtful, incisive Hawick stand-off in the 1970s, then coached club and district and finally Scotland.

the final of the prestigious Pacific tournament in Hong Kong and has won in Lisbon, while Borderers have appeared in guest teams in Sweden, Monaco, Australia and Saudi-Arabia. Ned Haig would never have believed it!

The difficulty in remembering the highlights of 'sevens' is that so much happens in a fleeting span of time that it's often hard to fix it all in sharp focus. On the other hand a dull tie, still only lasting the regulation 15 minutes, can seem an eternity. I can never be sure about the best individual tie I have seen — though Hawick's 1920s Houdini escape from 15-nil down to Dunfermline in a Jed final and still winning 18-15 takes some beating. It is easier to feel positive about the very best teams it has been one's good luck to see. Their record usually proves the point. For assembly-belt efficiency no seven, I think, has bettered Hawick's performance in 1966 and 1967 when they won 10 cups in succes-

Another young Lion to burst throught from the Borders. Gary Armstrong was 21 when first picked by Scotland in 1988. Later that season he was with the Lions in Australia. He could not have had a better mentor in a scrum-half's trade than his clubmate Roy Laidlaw who gained 47 caps, playing in the Grand Slam side and the World Cup.

sion. It all started where Greens like these things to start, at Netherdale, where they saw off two impressive guest sides, Cardiff and Loughborough Colleges. Thirty-nine ties later they were still unbeaten. At one stage they held all eight Border cups (Gala and

Craig Chalmers, the Melrose prodigy stand-off, gets his pass away despite a Kelso tackle. Capped in 1989 at only 20, he went on to become one of the youngest British Lions in the same year, winning a Test place against Australia. His father played for Melrose and Craig was spotted at primary school by that shrewd judge and former cap, Leslie Allan.

Melrose twice) plus an extra bauble they picked up with a scratch team at Huddersfield.

Gala's 'magnificent seven' of 1969-72 were undoubtedly Hawick's equal in most things, especially panache, and though they did not manage a grand slam of all the Border cups they reached 26 finals in a possible 30. This reflects the endless resource of a side containing such inimitable 'sevens' personalities as the three Browns (Arthur, Peter and Johnny), Duncan Paterson and Drew Gill. Yet their brilliance was echoed by Kelso soon afterwards when they made it to 11 of a possible 16 finals between 1973 and 1974. All this led to the full flowering of Kelso's 'sevens' flair in 1978 when, after nearly a century of trying, they at last won the Melrose Cup. Their achievement shines in my memory for the emergence of a precocious schoolboy, Roger Baird, who before long would be playing Test Rugby for the British Lions. He

A typical Andrew Ker try for Kelso against Hawick at Melrose 'sevens' in 1989.
He was on his way to his seventh Melrose medal in 15 appearances at the
classic tournament.

gained a Melrose medal at the first attempt. Many great players,
Jim Renwick, for instance, won just about everything else.
'Sevens' have always provided selectors with a valuable yardstick
of a young player's capabilities. There is no hiding place for the
player who cannot think on his feet, make every tackle tell, and
recognise out of the corner of his eye the faintest outline of an
overlap.

From a newspaper reporting point of view 'sevens' can be an
occupational hazard. You know when they will start but not
when they will finish. Put it all down to Ned Haig's decision to
settle drawn ties by 'first to score in extra time'. How long is extra
time? It can be anything from a few seconds after the second kick-
off till well into the night. I remember one marathon tournament

Gala's 'Magnificent Seven' after winning at Selkirk to maintain momentum which saw them through to the finals of 20 out of 24 successive Border tournaments. In 1970-71 they reached all eight Border finals. Back (left to right) — J. Brown, P. C. Brown, G. K. Oliver, J. Frame; front — J. Dobson, D. S. Paterson, A. R. Brown.

at Jed which ought to have been over by 7 p.m., tight enough with a newspaper edition to catch but possible provided all went well. The final was still in progress at 8.15. That was one result which did not get into the paper, which was printing by then.

There are many rum tales of extra time and the heavy wear and tear it has caused. At an early tournament at Melrose an enthralled crowd heard an imploring cry from the depths of a maul, 'For Gawd's sake somebody — anybody — score!' The cry came from a medical man in a green jersey. G. Mercer, Melrose, did what the good doctor ordered and stethoscopes were thankfully stowed away. On several occasions in the emergent

Burgeoning 'sevens' stars emerged in this Kelso team of 1973 which won all three Border autumn tournaments. Back (left to right) — I. Gillespie, J. Walker, T. Fleming, D. Wood; front — A. Ker, J. Chisholm, G. Fairbairn.

years the light faded before the sports could be played out to a conclusion, so the combatants had to assemble again in midweek.

Hawick have been involved in several of these punishing marathons. One of the most exhausting came at Kelso in 1947 when a semi-final against the home side ran to six periods of extra time. To everybody's huge relief, Hawick's included, Sandy Charters flopped over the Greens' line to bring blessed succour. This is often quoted as the longest 'sevens' tie but there was one within living memory — only just! — which managed to prolong the torture even more. This was a Langholm v Edinburgh Academicals tie at Mansfield in the 1920s which was only settled after seven periods of extra time. And that was only for starters since it was a first-round tie.

CHAPTER ELEVEN

Secret Uprising: Border League Blazed a Trail

IF at long and somewhat grudging last Twickenham has acknowledged a debt to Melrose and the Borders in the matter of 'sevens', it cannot yet be said that the Rugby world in general has followed the trail which the Border clubs blazed in the evolution of leagues. Few seem aware that competitive fifteen-a-side Rugby, as well as 'sevens', was watered and nourished within sight of the Eildons. Moreover this was accomplished under the beady eye of officialdom which did not like what it saw happening inside one of the Scottish districts. It is a curious story.

The Border League began on a seemingly low-key note in 1901-02, but no one can now say with certainty just how or why. The records are missing. Perhaps Border club officials, scraping around for funds in those impoverished days, had sensed how the cut-and-thrust of a 'sevens' afternoon could replenish their coffers. Perhaps they thought that if the same magic elixir could be spread to club games the crowds would roll in, as indeed they did. Perhaps they reasoned that players needed more than the one-off rivalry of the early club games and would react with enthusiasm to more tangible rewards. The trouble was that all this logic cut across the entrenched attitude of the powers that were. Nowadays it is hard to fathom why there should be this horror of leagues, yet there it was, in the same dire category as a flirtation with the Northern Union and broken time.

It must have taken a bit of courage, and cunning, by the Border clubs to set up their own league in that particular climate. At any rate they went ahead, and Hawick were the first to be entitled to call themselves champions of the Borders. It did not become the monopoly of Mansfield as has happened at later times in league history, Jedforest romping home in the next three seasons. It was already a properly organised competition from the start with a set of rules which the clubs have scarcely troubled to amend. Selkirk and Kelso were soon to be admitted to the original five but the unique feature of the Border League is that no one has ever been relegated. Even when Langholm dropped into Division Three of the National Leagues a place was still kept for them in the Border table. That's loyalty for you, and I suspect the need to cling together in the face of higher authority and to exert a traditional show of Border independence helps to explain why the league survived. Until comparatively recent times it was regarded with a decidedly frosty gaze from on high. I cannot vouch for it but byegone officials have told me when a Union visitation was expected, team pictures of Border League Champions would be turned to clubhouse walls. The same circumspection was observed in the presence of the great and the good at club dinners where a team would be warmly congratulated on achieving a success without specifying what it was — although everybody knew.

It is distinctly odd that the early minute books regarding the birthpangs of the Border League have long since disappeared. The first official accounts date from 10 years later in 1911. Strangely Melrose were champions in 1910-11 but the relevant pages in that club's minutes referring to the feat were mysteriously removed. Jedforest evidently had no inhibitions in 1906-07, the first year of the Border League Cup, when their president flourished aloft the trophy as he and his club captain were swept shoulder-high from Riverside to the town. Just as well that no television cameras were there to record the scene, otherwise in Edinburgh a few august fuses might conceivably have blown.

All I have been able to ascertain about the early years of the Border League is that meetings were generally held at the King's Arms, Melrose, a Rugby howff of some lineage, or at the Dryburgh, Newtown St Boswells. Presidents of the Border clubs took it in turn, for a year at a time, to preside over these meetings

One of the ablest officials who has ever served Border Rugby interests, John Robertson, Hawick, who was the South's secretary for 20 years in the '70s and '80s. During this time representative fixtures and tours hugely multiplied and National Leagues were introduced. Happily he continued as secretary of the Border League.

but the real running of the League was left largely to the secretary. This honorary official was nominally also secretary of the South District Union but he could never allow his left hand to know what his right hand was doing. League and Union representatives would meet in the same place on the same night, in a quorum composed of much the same people, but the secretary kept two minute books, one for the Union's eyes, the other

strictly for home consumption in the League. It must have been a
cloak-and-dagger business. Happily the Border League has been
served by a succession of secretaries who would probably have
carved out a substantial career for themselves in the diplomatic
service. Bob Hogg, who eventually became president of the
S.R.U., was one of the most acute of these, wearing his two hats
with vast aplomb from 1928 to 1949. Others who continued in the
same tricky tradition included Andrew Bunyan, Tom Carruthers,
Douglas Cockburn and the long-serving John Robertson who
piloted the Border barque through the choppy waters of the early
1970s and the introduction of the official leagues.

He and his predecessors could be allowed a wry smile when the
Union finally accepted that leagues were a good thing after all.
Even then the starting date was delayed for a year while Border
misgivings were placated. In the new framework the Border clubs
were implacably opposed to giving up their own old-established
league while some city pundits felt that the time had come for a
decent interment. That brought Border hackles up. A Border
view went like a tracer bullet across the city bows. The suggestion
was that maybe the other districts should organise their own
competitions on the same lines as the Borders and stage a knock-
out between the eight leading clubs at the end of the campaign.
That one was shot down but at least the South had made its point
and had also stressed the historic importance, not to mention the
financial significance, of the spring 'sevens'. In the end all was
amity but the Border clubs were made aware, as never before, of
just what they had started in their league.

Border flair for diplomatic dichotomy was demonstrated again
in the 1960s when, from out of the blue, came an invitation to
tour in South Africa. The Springboks wanted the South,
formidable at the time after giving the All Blacks a fright and
overcoming the Wallabies. What they got was the South under
another name, the Scottish Border Club. The same device was
used to allay any Union thoughts that the Borders might be
getting a bit above themselves. As a properly constituted club
they were on the same footing as the Co-optimists but they were
simply a Border side. Under the same banner they battled in later
years to a Hong Kong 'sevens' final. Global travel rewards many

Blowing a bit (excusably within a year of retirement!), Bill McLaren takes school coaching at Wilton Park, Hawick. Note that the celebrated commentator has a lady helping. During his long career as a teacher in Hawick, Bill recalls at least three women members of staff who were almost as enthusiastic about Rugby coaching as he was.

players at the top, or approaching it, nowadays but it was a great adventure in the '60s. The party was shrewdly managed by Jim Grieve (Kelso) and Andrew Bowie (Hawick), with Jim Telfer already showing his inspirational qualities as a tour captain. In playing results it was not a startling success, as in the circumstances it was never likely to be, but they won a game in a tough card of four and brought off a 23-all draw against the mighty Transvaal at Ellis Park which ranks as one of the battle honours in Border records.

These were happy, trouble-free days. The South were hugely popular and were dubbed 'The Ambassadors'. At their send-off for home Dr Danie Craven, South Africa's doyen of administrators, had this to say: 'The Borderers played their Rugby hard, they never tackled nor trampled on opponents unnecessarily, and they never queried decisions, not even with hard looks at the referee. You came, you did not conquer, but you have won the heart of every South African with whom you made contact.' You can hardly say fairer than that.

CHAPTER TWELVE

Seen From the Press Box:
The Funny Side of Rugby

RUGBY can be a funny game, especially when studied from the vantage point of the press box. One incident which still makes me chuckle, and, no doubt, a very few elderly fans turn choleric, took place at Mansfield during a Hawick-Gala Border League game in the mid-1950s. The referee was an Englishman, J.G. Mills. I cannot recall seeing him before nor, for that matter, since. His handling of the match seemed innocuous enough until he inexplicably blew for no-side. We looked at our watches. It could not be. There were at least 13 minutes of the second half to go. And he blew, too, with Gala leading precariously by 6-3.

Everyone agrees that the referee keeps the time and that the odd minutes added on for injury are entirely his own business. But to stop a game little more than half way through the second period was something different. On some sporting fields they might have been obliged to call out the National Guard. Nothing quite so dramatic happened at Mansfield but I do retain a vivid picture of Hawick's forceful official, 'Pud' Miller, tearing across the pitch at breakneck speed from the old pavilion, jacket flapping, gold watch in hand and a finger pointing menacingly at it. The unfortunate referee visibly cringed, and although it is clear that decisions once given cannot be rescinded, this one was. The referee re-started the game and played out the proper time. That was enough to give the bold G.D. Stevenson his cue and the Hawick centre jinked in for an equalising try. In the circumstances this was just about right.

A game which officially stops and starts again was pretty big news on any sports page and so it was that the Hawick happenings received the full treatment in the Sunday papers. Or, at least, all except one. My colleague Bob Coltherd had been ticked off by his sports editor a week earlier for devoting too much space to criticism of the referee. Bob took him at his literal word and failed to mention the extraordinary circumstances in which the local derby had been completed. 'I didn't want to appear to be criticising the referee', he told me. So readers of one Sunday paper never got to hear how Hawick purloined that notorious draw.

Of course not all the action takes place on the field. Even the bowels of the stand can regurgitate a story. One of my favourites comes from the Greenyards. A heavily concussed visiting prop was led by three local officials to the first-aid room. When he came round he woozily surveyed the trio and asked who they might be. The first was Sandy Gibson, the vet. The second was Derek Brown, the undertaker. And the third, grinning broadly, announced himself as Arthur Brown, the gravedigger. The casualty made a miraculous recovery!

Writing about Rugby is a lot easier than when I started. For one thing players are numbered, sometimes even correctly, and there are programmes to be picked up at the gate. Admittedly they are more pricey than the modest 3d four-pager for Murrayfield in the old days but at club level they can be helpful, even informative. Programmes did not come, with numbers, to Border grounds till 1953 when Hawick took the plunge. Incidentally at the same time the Greens also received permission from the local Council to use the town's coat-of-arms on their blazers, though whether the Lord Lyon knew of this one was never quite sure. Close identification of this kind between town and club became commonplace and rather set off the Border clubs from their city cousins.

Perhaps a bigger shift in reporting has been the personality cult, heavily frowned on long ago and now unashamedly encouraged. One could never seek an interview with a player or official. It simply was not done, smacking, no doubt, of professionalism. It

No Border Rugby player and administrator has gone further in the game than George ('Dod') Burrell of Gala seen here (left) with the club president, Dave Brydon, at the opening of the Burrell Room at Netherdale. 'Dod's' litany of success covers Scottish caps at full back, international referee, chairman of the Scottish selectors, manager of two overseas Scotland tours, manager of the 1977 British Lions in New Zealand and finally chairman of the International Rugby Board. His unique collection of Rugby souvenirs from his worldwide travels has now found a home with his old club.

was sometimes hard enough to check on who was playing. Changes might be chalked on a board at the gate and still legible on a dry day. Loudspeakers had not come to test our eardrums. Some club officials were more co-operative than others. The general tone was set from on high where the brooding presence at Murrayfield of the Union's formidable secretary, J. Aikman Smith, discouraged close contact with the press. We were tolerated — just.

Most members of the Rugby press corps of the '20s and '30s wrote under pseudonyms. Charlie Stuart, the old Glasgow High cap, was for long the doyen of them all as 'Touch Judge' of the dear old *Bulletin*. Some of the pen-names were quite exotic. I liked the patriarchal Diogenes who cast a beady eye over the Murrayfield scene from his eyrie at the back of the stand for the *Evening News*. I especially valued the friendship of that wise old bird, Gaberlunzie, who had seen the very first international at Raeburn Place and who wrote for many years for the *Daily Record*, a somewhat more chaste paper then than now.

The general approach seemed to be to regard Rugby reporting as not much removed from theatre criticism. One sat through the show, thought about it and wrote about it. One certainly didn't wait till the curtain fell and then dash behind the scenes to get an instant reaction from actors and producer. So many of these quotes are totally predictable anyway. One observed a certain decorum with regard to the members of the cast. Players were known by their initials, never by anything so chummy as first names. It was G.P.S. Macpherson or J.B. Nelson. The Andy's and the Jim's were to come later.

Getting copy to one's paper, too, had different problems. When I began it was not unusual for stories to be transmitted by telegram. The Post Office granted a special concession to newspapers. The rate was 60 words for a shilling, the words being inscribed in neat boxes on a typical Civil Service form. This compared with a penny a word for ordinary commercial traffic. One was supplied with a book of passes to cover the transmission, white for ordinary news, pink if it had to be sent at the full penny a word rate and was concerned with something so momentous as a naval mutiny or a royal assassination. It was important that one flicked out the right colour of pass otherwise some startled city sub-editor might press the alarm bells on receiving a pink message and discover that Earlston had beaten Walkerburn by a penalty goal. Post Offices were open till lateish on a Saturday night and on Sunday mornings. Many a story was dashed off on a P.O. counter prompted by a clerk who had also been at the game. The extension of the telephone service has changed all that but the phone can be a weak link in the chain — even the newest cordless contraptions have to compete on occasion with the crackle from the Twickenham car park.

Bob Burrell, 'Dod's' younger brother, who followed the succession of Gala's international referees. He was groomed by the renowned Sandy Dickie who was also a Gala midfield back. Bob is a brilliant raconteur. He has even been invited to Central Africa just to speak at a Rugby dinner. One of his memories is of his first international assignment in Dublin. Just a week earlier the Nelson Pillar in O'Connell Street had been toppled in the 'troubles'. Pinned to his bedroom door on the morning of the match Bob found a picture of the fallen Nelson and the scrawled message. 'It was him last week, it could be you this!' Quite coincidentally, Bob adds, Ireland won!

I used to dread Dublin. At one time there was no reverse-call system between the Republic and the U.K. so one had to organise a phone near the ground through which the paper could ring you at the pre-arranged time. Easier said than done. The *Sunday Post* once advised me that their Dublin freelance correspondent would fix me up with a phone and Glasgow would call me at 6 p.m. This sounded fine until I stepped off the morning boat at the North Wall and tried to verify the arrangement. The Dublin contact man wasn't even in the phone book himself. I rang a friend at the *Irish Times*. He knew him but wasn't much help. 'He'll probably be in a pub by now. He usually goes round half-a-dozen of a Saturday morning but I wouldn't know where you'd likely find him.'

With a premonition of doom I filled my pockets full of Irish shillings which at that time were slightly larger than the U.K. variety. I ran my man to ground at Lansdowne Road and demanded to know where I would find the all-important phone. A James Joycean character, he gave me a conspiratorial wink and led me, a shade unsteadily, to the turnstile at the railway end and pointed away down the road to a distant call-box. 'That's it,' he said. Well, if that was the number he had passed through to Glasgow it would suit me since I have phoned from some pretty odd places in my time, though I did hope no garrulous old soul would monopolise the box with endless gossip.

After the match I wrote my piece and wandered off to the call-box with time in hand. I liked the look of it. It was spanking new, smelling of emerald paint, and it had a glossy black shelf, coinbox and the two buttons, A and B. I settled down to flip through my notes waiting for the phone to ring. Then I broke out in a sweat. The phone box had everything except a phone. This was the cue to switch to the alternative plan. I nipped across the road to the nearest pub, Irish pubs always being provided with public phones. This one dangled from the wall in a well-filled main bar. 'Go ahead', said the barman when I asked if I might use the phone. I didn't dare tell him how long I might be. That he'd find out later. Anyway it all went well, Glasgow was there, and they could hear me. I remember one venerable Dublin character coming out from behind his frothing pot of black stout to watch the silver cascading like a mountain brook into the maws of the coin-box. 'Now tell me, sir', he said as I hung up. 'What paper was that for?' 'Oh, that was for the *News of the World* — you'll read it tomorrow.' His mouth opened wide. He crossed himself. That was the paper which was on the bishops' banned list at the time. As the paper itself might have said, I made my excuses and left.

CHAPTER THIRTEEN

Lament for a Lost Line: Rugby Trips No More

FEW names have been more reviled among branch-line railway enthusiasts than Beeching. The good doctor did more than merely leave the Borders out on a limb when in the 'sixties he dismembered the Waverley Line which snaked through the district from Edinburgh to Carlisle: he ensured that Rugby trips would never be the same again. Younger followers can only guess at what they have missed. Their dads and grand-dads will lovingly recall the camaraderie, the convenience, and the unbelievable economy of those biennial train trips to Twickenham, Cardiff or Dublin. Somehow Paris always seemed just beyond reach.

Posters advertising Rugby Specials were posted in the Border towns many weeks before the match, allowing a timely interval for wifely scruples to be overcome. The trains set off from Edinburgh with a rather exclusive quota of city supporters who had discovered what a bargain it was, even if they stayed discreetly quiet about their mode of travelling when business colleagues spoke of flying down for the match. The first stop was at Galashiels where the platform was lined with the first phalanx of fellow travellers and also and invariably by a goodly gang of envious friends who had just come to see them off.

The ritual was repeated at Melrose and St Boswells before the biggest crowd clambered aboard at the last stop, Hawick. By now the carriages, the corridors and the capacious buffet car were rocking to rich Rugby crack. Everybody was heading for the same place, so there was only one possible topic — the match. The old campaigners among us would go in search of a compartment beyond earshot of the buffet where, with any luck, we might snatch some fitful sleep. I remember Bill McLaren and me finding one all to ourselves on a homeward trip from Swansea and enjoying almost the luxury of a sleeper. When we nodded off we could still hear a Welsh porter calling his incomprehensible station. When we stirred we could just hear 'Hyke', and Bill was off the train in a flash. How effortless it all was.

Apart from virtual door-to-door delivery by British Rail the Border spectators reaped a rich dividend in value. Travel in four countries, for instance, on land and by sea, and all for just under a pound. You doubt me? Here's what you got for nineteen shillings return from Gala: South to Carlisle and across north-west England and Wales to Holyhead; swop the warmth of the train for the knife-edged chill of the ferry crossing to Dun Laoghaire; then a short cheerful train journey up to Dublin and the welcoming crackle of log fires in the Shelbourne Hotel. After the match the process was reversed and one was back in the Borders for a late Sunday breakfast.

There were, of course, other trips, other Rugby Specials. Various ways were on offer for the jaunt to Ireland. My favourite was aboard the boat from Glasgow's Broomielaw on the Friday night, a substantial ship's breakfast alongside the North Wall in the dawn, followed by a leisurely morning to sniff the turf reek along the Liffey and quaff a Guinness before heading off to Lansdowne Road. There was an alternative sail from Glasgow to Belfast before rattling south over the border in the oddly named United Irishman, a slower, bumpier Flying Scot. I covered the last match in Belfast at Ravenhill, more an intimate club ground than an international stadium. By the mid-fifties it could have been filled several times over.

Scotland lost that match and lost, too, in a farewell appearance at St Helen's, Swansea. I recall both of these discarded international grounds with genuine affection. Swansea, perhaps, especially for our Rugby Special driving through the Celtic twilight of dimly perceived stations down the spine of Wales. The ground was a delight. If matters were going badly one could always avert one's gaze to the fine sweep of Swansea Bay and the pounding surf of the Bristol Channel. By comparison the straight journey to the clattering saucepans of Cardiff Arms Park was more to be endured than enjoyed. Despite the tumult I will say that Cardiff is the most Rugby-minded city of them all. You are never left in doubt that it is a big day — and that Wales are going to win. Official programme sellers are out and about hours before the kick-off. Elsewhere programmes are sold only inside the ground. The local evening papers come out during the morning with fat supplements telling you everything about the match and its combatants except the score, though here again the result is obvious — ain't it, Dai? I suppose life must go on normally somewhere in Cardiff on an international day but to those of us who travelled down on a Border Rugby Special it always seemed as though routine existence had been suspended for 24 hours while 30 young men pursued an oval ball. It always helped, too, that the Arms Park was within punting distance of the railway and bus stations. Contrast that with the far trek to Twickenham or Parc des Princes.

It can be forgotten that the Waverley Line and its feeders also brought most spectators to the big Rugby games in the Borders in the pre-Beeching era and, of course, to the sports. If some nemesis should unaccountably overtake Hawick at the Greenyards, one could be sure there would be a wag to insist that someone ought to pass the word up to the engine-driver high on the embankment overlooking the ground and warn him to get steam up. In point of fact the message was probably unnecessary since that railway worthy was very likely keeping an attentive eye on what was happening down below and reasoning that most of his passengers would presently be flooding back to the station.

The railway ran specials to all the sports, even Earlston and Langholm. It was a marvellously matey way of going. It isn't the same by coach and even less so by car. The Border Rugby Specials brought all kinds of supporters together and made of them a grand democratic mix. By the time we had sorted out the current match or sports we could always turn to the state of the Border League or the rumoured sighting of a scout from the Rugby League. Especially when we lost, an international journey by rail underlined the adage that it is often better to travel than to arrive. The Specials, after all, were just a Rugby clubroom on wheels.

CHAPTER FOURTEEN

Where Now? Rugby Faces Up to Change

ANYONE skimming through these pages might imagine that Rugby in the Borders has made a fairly painless progress through the last dozen decades or so. So it has, but it would be daft to ignore the cosmic changes which are now at work. In Scotland the watershed may well have been the acceptance of a national league with seven grades, and all that this implies in tension. It is a long way from the cosy arrangement of the Border League. Clubs can climb from sea level to the summit as Stirling County did, or plunge almost as dizzily as several of the revered names of yesteryear have done. Sentiment is out. Results are in. This may be logical enough in most sports but Rugby has rather preened itself on being a cut above the rest, the very bastion of the pure Corinthians. It can hardly claim to be that now, though to be fair the introduction of leagues in Scotland was achieved with less hassle and rancour than, say, in England or Wales.

One of the effects has been to switch emphasis from club to country. A good rating in the international championship and a good run in the World Cup are taken as the measure of a country's success. Clubs, if they are not careful, can become mere feeders for the higher echelons of the game. This would be a great pity. One of the distinguishing features of Rugby has always been the way that the members run their clubs — or at least they elect the people who do and in many cases lend them a willing hand. This is in stark contrast to the 'them and us' ambience of the privately owned professional football club.

It's mine! Serge Blanco, the colourful French full back, who was born in South America, holds aloft the Melrose Cup after it crossed the Channel for the first time at the Centenary tournament of 1983. Behind him is the Melrose president, Jack Dun.

It is always heartening to see Rugby men ploughing something back into the game. Hugh McLeod, for instance, won 40 caps with Hawick, then became club and Border League president. After that he went uncomplainingly back to the mundane job of selling tickets for the car park. 'Somebody has to do it.' The best clubs are nearly always served by the best officials. It is no coincidence that the worldwide fame of Melrose Sevens has been watered and nourished down the years by such dedicated folk as Bob Brown, Jimmy Johnston, Tom Wight, Jack Dun and Stuart Henderson. In the 1920s secretaries wielded even more autonomy than now. I remember a kenspeckle Selkirk official, Bob Mitchell, laying his plans for his club's first win over Hawick, something that was needed to establish senior status. Bob heard that Charlie Usher, the current Scottish skipper and an inspirational leader of men, would be spending the weekend on a fishing trip on the Ettrick. He cranked up his old jalopy and sped off to see the great man. He returned with the news that, yes, Usher would lead the Selkirk pack against Hawick. He led them with such cyclonic force that Bob's prophecy was fulfilled and Selkirk did indeed beat the mighty Greens for the first time in a Border League match. There were the inevitable growls and hints of sharp practice though not, it is fair to say, from the Hawick club. There was nothing in the rules to prevent Charlie Usher from hooking a Hawick sea trout among his clean-run salmon. The return match became highly charged as by now Usher had returned to the city. Bob Mitchell had no more aces up his sleeve, or so Hawick thought, except one. 'Just think, Charlie's leading you out at Mansfield', he declaimed, and Selkirk believed him for they beat Hawick again. This double would be recalled for many years to come when scores had reverted to what Hawick would equably regard as the norm.

Despite some initial difficulties in marrying national and Border League fixtures the problems now seem to have been overcome, and with goodwill there is no obvious reason why the oldest Rugby competition in the world should not keep rumbling along for many seasons to come. Even an incipient threat of professionalism would not affect it. The towns are the right size for their kind of competition and local loyalties are strong. If the fifteen-a-side prospects look reasonably secure one cannot in all honesty say the same about the 'sevens'. It is odd that the recession — for we have to accept it as such — should date from what was undoubtedly the short game's finest hour, the Melrose

Allez France! The jubilant French Barbarians and their coach and officials after a champagne performance to crown the Melrose celebrations.

Centenary Sevens. The 1983 draw was enlarged to 24 teams and the first tie kicked off at 11.30 a.m. Around 6.30, as always, two teams lined up for the final. Six hours' scintillating Rugby for your money — some bargain! The British Barbarians and the French Barbarians were seeded in the glittering draw. Royal High School (remember them?) struck the first blow by eliminating the Baa-Baa's, Les Cusworth and all.

The French Barbarians were made of sterner stuff. With a seven which included such legendary heroes as Blanco, Esteve, Joinel and Dintrans, they spirited the Melrose Cup out of the country for the first time. In a curious way 'sevens' became the victim of its own success. The other four tournaments on the Border spring circuit found it increasingly hard to live up to the Melrose excellence and the gap became embarrassingly wide. An effort has been made to make one or two of the others as attractive as they used to be but the uncertainties caused by English and Welsh cup competitions and the regularity with which Scotland and other Home countries go on early summer tours have syphoned off some of the personalities and made it harder to organise a first-rank tournament. The answer might lie in a more selective draw. Are 16 teams really needed unless they are out of the top drawer? One of the most entertaining afternoons of 'sevens' I can recall was provided at Kelso in the late 1940s when the entry was limited to eight clubs — the seven Border sides plus Cardiff Training College — and there wasn't a dull moment.

A more basic answer probably lies in the change which has overtaken the fifteen-a-side game in the wake of the Australian dispensation which eliminates direct kicking to touch outside the 22-metre lines. This has helped club games to flow as they seldom did in the earlier days of 'sevens'. After a winter of watching teams creep up and down the touchline it was a blessed relief to switch to the infinitely more fluid 'sevens'. Now, of course, a touch of 'sevens' play can flicker in almost any fifteen-a-side match. In this respect things are not what they used to be.

Nevertheless for the aficionado there is nothing quite like Border Sevens. The tournaments usually come at the right time of year when spring is burgeoning. They offer a farewell to winter and often a farewell to players who have earned the respect and adulation of Border spectators. Some, indeed, will follow the example of sundry craggy characters of the past and on the last day at Walkerburn will hurl their boots over the touchline and into the Tweed.

Maybe I should do the same.

Index